Delusions of a Rock N Roll Messiah
The Further Adventures of Texas Guitar Legend
Nathon Dees

This is the Second Book in The Texas Guitar Legend Series. In Delusions of a Rock n Roll Messiah you will join in the Adventure as the Rev. Nathon Dees leaves Jaco, Costa Rica to returns to the United States of Confusion, Recovers from Mental Illness and Ascends only to uncover the Greatest Conspiracy ever told with him Right in the middle of it. From playing Live Rock n Roll Guitar at Bike rallies to being thrown into a Government Maximum Security Psycho Ward and being stripped of all rights for no crime and no reason only to escape the Marshall Law New World Order that was taking place in the U.S. and return to Exile in Central America.

Chapter One
Goodbye Pura Vida

After spending four years living on the beach in a small coastal Village in Costa Rica, I had decided that it was a time for a change. I was till severely mentally ill but I had learned to overcome some of the more severe symptoms of my schizoaffective disorder. My daughter Natolie was already back in the States living with a friend Michael Klumpp and my son Aaron was fixing to be eighteen and wanted to move back to the United States so that he could finish school and get a driver's license.

About this time I heard from my old buddy Art Napoli who was now living in Arizona of all places. He simply asked me if I still wanted to play guitar and I said that I would love to be in a band again or to come play guitar with him. I made arrangements for my dad to take over my business in Costa Rica then Aaron, Don Cool and I left our super cool surfer village where we were safe from society and returned to the United States of Confusion.

You have got to understand why I left the states in the first place. Everything that I had been taught to believe in was a Lie and everyone that I knew back in the states was part of the conspiracy. Mania and depression themselves are very difficult to cope with, even in a controlled environment, like back in the US, how would I ever be able to adjust to the oppression and opposition that I would be met with back in the States.

When I arrived at the International Airport Houston Airport (IAH), on my lay over to Arizona, my ex wife Athea was there. She ran to me and held me like there was no tomorrow. We wept as we held each other tight then she asked me if there was any way that I could change my plans to come stay with her so that we could be together once more. I painfully told her no. For one, she had never supported me in my struggle with mental illness and still thought I was demon possessed and not mentally ill. More importantly, she was not the one that invited me to come back to the States or offered me a job, Art did. I caught my connecting flight and was on my way to Arizona to begin a new adventure and see what was next in life.

Art had always been a real player and this time he had once again out done himself. The gig in Arizona was a good deal so I started work the day after I got there making $30 per hour cash. I went from living on my small government check and having no money for years to making several thousand dollars a week instantly. I was adjusting to things the best way that I could but the reality of the matter was I was completely freaked out. Art had to basically take care of me in the since that I did not really even want to talk to other people and as long as Art took me to work, fed me lunch and told me the job detail I needed to work I was fine and could function. Here is the catch Art is bipolar too and he lives in a world of mania. He is always swinging a deal or making something happen. Well it turns out that the reason that we were in Arizona was because Art's old girlfriend Tammy had been transferred there. Well, that was OK, Tammy was super cool and she was my friend as well but that just wasn't enough for Art so he moved his other girlfriend, Sheila, in to Arizona to hang out with us too. Now, how long do you think it took for the two girls to figure out that he was seeing them both again in another state? Not long enough.

When the, double life double girlfriend, fiasco exploded on Art and the high paying construction job came to an end it was time to go back to Texas with our winnings and start our new Rock Band Called Ten Foot Hammer.

Chapter Two
Hello Texas

Aaron and I showed up in Austin Texas with an old 93 Ford F-150 that we had bought in Arizona from Art and enough cash to last a month or so. Well, since I had been a successful business owner, built and owned my own homes and was self employed I had no rental history, no employment records, no source of income, and no references. I had just spent the last three and a half years living on a beach in a third world country battling schizophrenia and I could not find a place to stay in Austin. Aaron and I went back to our almost home town of Dripping Springs Texas. The government had built some low income Apartments called the Springs but since there really aren't that many low income families in Dripping Springs because they can't afford to live there, the apartments were really kind of nice, especially compared to what we had been used to in Costa Rica. The lady at the "Springs" told us that she would give us a lease if my mom would cosign for us since we were home folk. Well this was the best news that we had got since we returned to the states. Aaron got a job at the school and I was traveling to Austin everyday doing odds and ends stuff for money and playing with a couple of bands trying to get something going. Meanwhile, Art was auditioning every drummer in town and trying to get something going with whoever he could when he introduced me to Guy Elder. Guy was cool enough but he was kind of a poser. I mean he was real enough and he was a bad ass drummer and road a Harley and was otherwise a really cool dude but he was a little drama queen and thought a little more highly of himself than he should when he wasn't beating himself up. Another fucked up Bi Polar Quasi religious Christian freak. Well, in order to get Guy to play drums for Art's " Ten Foot Hammer" band I agreed to play bass and Sing for Guy's band "Triple Tree", a 70's & 80"s, classic rock cover band. Art wanted to play dropped D southern party music and hit the Local Austin scene but Guy was fed up with gigging bars and wanted to focus on motorcycle rallies and parties. Hell, I didn't care, I just wanted to jam. Well, after several months of preparation for both bands everything fell through on me. Our friend Ahmed Garcia was going to play lead for Triple Tree but Ahmed had already been working on his own solo hippie music and for years and was trying to manipulate Guy into playing for him. Well, Guy was secretly trying to manipulate Ahmed to play for his band instead and well Art he was trying to manipulate Guy through me to do his will so that he could have more than one drummer available that knew the material. So everyone fucked everyone else over because of their own selfish ambition and pride and everything blew up in my face. At the time I didn't really know how chicken shit Guy was so when he offered to take Aaron and I with him to College Station to continue with Triple Tree I jumped on it. I am thankful for what I achieved working with Guy and I had some good times in College Station but in retrospect I will have to admit that Guy his Buddy Chris and most of the people that I met in College Station are the biggest bunch of back stabbing liars that I have ever met in my entire life. It took three years of living with Guy and Jamming with him and Chris to realize the depth of their deception and lies. Nearly everything that they had told me was a lie. They knew every one in every band and were friends with Pantera and had toured the world. Ninety percent of it was all bullshit. It turns out that they were make up wearing fagot posers from the 90's that had only played locally and experienced very limited success. Hell they could not even book a gig, never showed up for practice, could not remember their parts, and did not do anything but criticize each other. They both sucked. Hell I grew as a musician because of them. Their lack of professionalism forced me to step up to the plate. I was originally just going to play bass and now I was doing the sound, lights set up and take down, playing lead and rhythm while doing the lead vocals. Chris was so dumb that he could not even remember which parts that he sang from gig to gig so I always had to sing his parts too. I was doing AC/DC, Judas Priest, ZZ Top, you name it we played it. It was all top 40 classic Rock and I played it with integrity.

When the gig went well it was all Aaron and I. I was the front man and it was my show.
Guy and Chris were really holding me back and it was time for me to go in a different direction.
(Art showed back up in the Picture and was willing to do the Ten foot Hammer gig again so we picked up and went back to Austin to hit the bar scene and play every week end.)

The House where we were living in College Station was a huge old mansion that we had rented from some friends of Guy's after we remodeled it. When we decided to move to Austin the same people had a house there so we remodeled it for them and moved in it. I had been seeing my psychologist the whole time that I had been back in the States. I was seeing Dr. Joan Clayton the head Psychologist at the VA Hospital and we had a very good working relationship. I was taking meds and sleeping most of the time and doing everything that I could to remain balanced. I also had enrolled in a program at Texas A&M University and was seeing a psychology student there named Anna. I had enrolled in a program called DARS (Department of rehabilitative services or something like that) and they were paying for me to go to college.

So let's get the gist of this. I was still pretty messed up. Still somewhat delusional and schizoaffective while rebounding back and forth from meds to no meds. I was going to college and taking psychology classes and playing in the band at night. The rest of the time I was either asleep or a brain dead zombie on the meds. We never had any money and we all really didn't get along very well. Art worked hard all day and when he came home before a gig the first thing that did was start a fight with Guy by telling him what a worthless piece of shit that he was. This always set the mood. Now Guy is all pissed off at Art and I have to load up all of the shit because they won't speak. This was and still is Arts modes' apparati.

He blames it on me and we both blame it on the Army and my dad Byron for making us into such assholes but when dealing with stupid people you almost have to subjugate them and beat them down or you can't use them. If someone is not your equal and you are in authority over them the only way to make them respect you is to make them fear you or dread you. I understand the concept completely but at this point in my life I am still looking for equals and not followers as it were. I don't want the stress and the power struggles and I out rank most people in intellect and ability any way so the last thing that you want to do with me is pull rank and start barking orders. At this point in life one of two things are going to happen I will smile at you and turn and walk away never to return or we will have a violent altercation. I tend to walk away quite often now days.

Chapter Three
College Station Crazy Train

The house in College Station was nearly 3000 square foot but it was old so no one wanted it. The fireplace was nearly six feet long and the house had huge rooms. Guy had his room down stairs that he only came out of for work or to jam. He was a recluse and always kept to himself. Art and Shelia were staying in the living room in front of the fire place during the winter and Natolie and Aaron had their own rooms upstairs. I also let Natolie's friend from school live with us so I could help her get through school. The music studio was the largest room in the house so I chose the smallest room. There was an office off to the side of the kitchen just big enough for a bed. This was my home. Ever since I lost my Quarter of a million dollar house in Wimberley, Texas that I had built for Athea, I had become a minimalist. So, if I don't have anything of value then you don't have anything worth taking from me. In Costa Rica I let Aaron and Natolie sleep in the house with air conditioning and I slept on the porch on a cot under a mosquito net. When I moved into the hostel I again took basically a closet and made a room out of it, more like a prison cell than a room. In my room I had a bed, a guitar and a surf board, this is where I found comfort. I would have coffee in the morning and take Natolie to school in an old Volvo that someone had given me. When Natolie was going to graduate even though I was poor I pulled all of my resources and did a big remodeling job in Austin then I bought her a Mercedes Benz 350SL Grey car and restored it. The car was a beautiful and worth a lot of money so I felt like I had finally dealt justice to Natolie. I had helped her get through high school and bought her a nice expensive car even though I was a mentally handicapped musician that she did not approve of. It only took two weeks for Natolie to totally destroy the car in a collision. She took an unprotected left hand turn at a four way intersection and was wiped out by another car. She wasn't injured severely but it still cost me nearly ten thousand dollars and a car that I had just rebuilt. My mom helped me to get Natolie another car and she soon moved out and went out on her own.

I had been talking to my ex wife Athea from time to time and we were getting along OK but she still refused to accept any responsibility for our divorce, she was still unwilling to accept my illness and insisted that the problems were spiritual in nature. I had known and loved Athea since I was thirteen years old and I just never really understood what a liar that she really was. She was in church every time that the doors were open and spent every day reading the bible and quoting scriptures. Yet, even though I was not good enough for her to love, she had sex with me every time I saw her. I never advanced on her sexually, every time we where alone she would have her way with me. Hell, nothing had changed, that is why I married her, that's what she was behind my back while we were together and that's what she was doing now. In fact she even had another boy friend that she lied to me about while she was seeing me and was pregnant with his Child..

Everything in her life was a lie and it took me nearly thirty years to understand how deep the rabbit hole went. The amount of time, love and devotion I had thrown away on this individual in the name of love. What a fool I was for believing in love one more time.

Chapter Four
Reprogramming my Cognition

Wrecked cars, broken relationships, deception and lies, everyone that I was involved with had major character flaws, lacked morality and acted as if they were normal. Hell, I was the one that was mentally ill I was the one seeing a doctor and going to counseling.

Everyone claimed to be a Christian and go to church "except for Art" and they were all liars that had no foundation of truth in their lives. Guy would lie to everyone that he talked to on the phone and make up excuses for every short Cumming in his life. Chris was a lying instigating bastard that wouldn't know the truth if it hit him.
Athea bless her heart was the biggest nut case liar that I had ever met and I had been in love with her since I was thirteen years old. Art was just a Bi polar psychopath on drugs, at least he had an excuse!

OK, so, I am the damaged one. I have schizophrenia, am I broken and can't be a part of society or have a job or a future? I am the only one with any moral character at all. I had walked away from religion time and time again in search of ultimate truths. I had shunned and refuted anything in my life that seemed to lead me in the wrong direction. I took great strides to avoid drugs and alcohol even though I was very susceptible to them. Sure, I was mentally ill but I was not morally ill. I still knew the difference between right and wrong.

Natolie directed me to a book Called "Cognitive Behavioral Therapy for Dummies" I read it and reprogrammed my mind in one week.

I felt that Natolie and Aaron secretly despised me and blamed me for all or the shortcomings in their lives. Guy was a complete liar and a back biting gossip queen, Chris was a liar and a Dirtbag " Guy Loved him and Chris could do no wrong in Guy's eyes". Everyone that said that they were my friend in College Station turned on me, robbed me and slandered me because of the lies that Guy and Chris had told them and I was eventually railed out of town.

When I finally left College Station there were eight false police reports with my name on them and I had done nothing to anyone and they were all lies.

You see after Ten Foot Hammer broke up I went back to Costa Rica to visit my dad.
Before I left my son Aaron had spoke to me and said " Hey pop I know that you have some problems and so do I but you still know how to do things because your dad taught you, I am twenty one years old now and I can't get a job making tacos." I had been feeding, clothing, and providing shelter for Aaron but since I was not in business anymore and not running jobs like I had my whole life I had never apprenticed Aaron on the Job like my father had so at twenty one he basically had no trade skills what so ever so when I returned home from Costa Rica I went to work to try and build a future for Aaron. After all, my son Aaron is the only one that had not lied to me or betrayed me since I had returned to the United States.

When I returned home from my visit with my dad in Costa Rica I left Austin and moved to Bryan Texas which was next to College Station and moved into another house that I had previously remodeled.
I went to work immediately. The day after I returned I was on a job. I rebuilt a porch and re roofed a house and then the next week Aaron and I built a car port while Guy was lining out a room addition on a restaurant. The whole time that I had been working with Guy for the last three years I let him think that he knew something and I tried to support him and make him feel better about himself, well that time was over and I was going to be Nathon again. When I took over the job and started doing all the work and dealing with the customer first hand Guy freaked out. He really did not know or understand who or what that I really was. He thought that I was a mentally ill handy man and did not realize that I was a professional craftsman and a home builder so when I stepped up to the plate it was embarrassing for him because he could not be the big man any more. I ran circles around him on the job and everything that I did was correct and finished and nearly everything that he did was flawed. Like I said before Guy was a poser so everything that he ever accomplished was on the heels of someone else. Well this time his dumb ass was exposed and everyone could see his folly in the open. I realized that because of my decision to try again and be somebody so that I could help Aaron, it

was going to destroy my relationship with Guy and that I really would be on my own for the first time in years. I had to come up with a plan and find a way to start and run a business that could sustain Aaron and provide him an income.

Chapter Five
I awoke the Genius Again

At this time I had been rebuilding an old guitar that someone had given me and I was building a face plate for it out of wood. When I finished the face plate I realized that there would be a market for such a product but I knew that in order to mass produce such an item I would need a CNC machine. I went to the internet and much to my dismay the CNC machines that I would need to start my business started at about five thousand dollars and I did not have that kind of capitol. I only had a couple of thousand dollars to live on off of the Restaurant job and I did not have Guy to help me anymore. That is when I saw a web site on building your own CNC machine and I started studying and researching the machines. Within a week I had completely invented designed and fabricated my own CNC machine and the computer hardware necessary to run it. I taught myself auto cad and tool path programming over the internet and I was up and running. My machine worked great and I was on my way to being a successful business man again for the first time since I had been diagnose with mental illness . When I built the CNC machine I rebuilt myself. I chartered a nonprofit business and got all of my tax ID's and permits and leased a booth at the local flea market where I would start selling my goods and taking orders for custom name plates and artwork that Aaron and I were making on the CNC machine. We were on our own and making money.

I came up with a plan to buy an old church in town and turn it into a trade school where I could get government grants to teach trades to people with no education. I was making a deal with the courts to get community service labor so I could repair houses for the elderly in the community and repair homes for single mothers and low income families. Aaron and I designed then I had invented a new kind of vaporizer that allowed you to inhale Pot or tobacco without any carcinogens that would basically prevent cancer from smoking. I had two gas models and three electric models. Once again I was taking over my world and I was on top of my game. That is when the shit hit the fan once more.

Chapter Six
Marshall Law Speed Trap

This is the actual letter that I wrote to the Judge, Police Chief, and Captain of the Bryan DPS after I happened in to a Speed trap.

On the night of 4/14/2011 at Approximately 0130 Hrs I was traveling south bound on SH 6 Traveling from Jerrell, Texas in rout to 4207 Woodcrest, Bryan Texas my place of residence. I had traveled to Miss Annie's house at the request of a friend because a contractor had stolen approx $ 12,000. From an elderly lady and I was asked to give a construction analysis and do the much needed repairs at no cost to the Lady. I was traveling at a sustained rate of 60 miles per hour as indicated by my speedometer in my black 1993 Ford F150. In the clear night sky I could see a State Trooper's LED Lights on the right hand side of the road from about a mile and a half away so I started to decelerate. I knew that I was approaching a town so I looked for a radar sign or a Orange reduced speed ahead sign. There were none. Then I saw on the left hand side of the road a fifty miles per hour sign (that was gone when I returned) and behind it a black and white patrol car hiding in obscurity. As a soldier I immediately realized that this was an ambush (speed trap) and I started to pull over before the officer even turned on his lights and pulled out. The first thing that I noticed was that the DPS on the right was in front of a Champaign colored step side pickup with aluminum wheels which is not S.O.P for officers (rear end collisions). I pulled in front of Officer Cox squad car and put both of my hands outside the window as if I were a captive officer in a hostile environment and awaited the arrival of officer Lightfoot who was still turning around. When Officer Lightfoot approached my vehicle I gave him my name rank and business and told him that the only way that I could get my Insurance and registration was if he would allow me to get out of the truck and go to the other side because the glove box was obstructed. He allowed me to do so. After I gave him the information I walked to the center of the back of my truck between the patrol cars (violation of S.O.P. for rear end collision) and assumed the position of parade rest until the time that I was released from custody.

After reviewing my spotless driving and criminal record Officer Lightfoot said that I was a liar, that Jerrell was not as far as I said it was and that he was going to get to the bottom of this and started taking everything out of mu truck. He responded in glee when he retrieved my one gallon jug of communion wine that was located in the far right floor board and was completely inaccessible. He " what do we have hear" I asked for a field sobriety test and was denied, I asked for a breath test and was denied, I asked for a blood test and was denied.

Then he said "let's see what else we can find" and began removing the hundreds of items that volunteers had put in my truck as donations to my ministry.

Officer Cox of the DPS stood beside me and watched but he never spoke a word. Officer Cox was squared away and treated me with the respect of my office. He also bore the cross of my savior proudly displayed on his uniform.

Officer Lightfoot with the swagger of a drunken brawler then magically appeared with a one inch glass jelly jar that contained a small amount of Green vegetated biomaterial that he claimed was Cannabis Sativa and placed it on the bed of my truck in plain view of Officer Cox patrol video. He had no gloves on, he took no pictures, there were no fingerprints, there was no lab sample, and he never opened the Jar. Officer Lightfoot made railing accusations against me and accused me of being a dope head. When I was asked why a pastor would have pot in his truck I responder Verbatim "Sir possession of Cannabis Sativa is illegal in Texas but if I had any it would be because I have Bi Polar Disorder and cannabis sativa contains delta 9 tetrahydrocanabinol and is a serotonin inhibitor that blocks nuerotransmision and prevents mania but that is not my pot". Officer Cox then asked me if I had smoked any marijuana and I responded "Sir I have no pipe, I have no Bong, I have no papers and I have no lighter but I guess that I could eat it. Officer Cox smiled.

Officer Lightfoot then explained to me that he would take the pot and not report it and would just give me a drug paraphernalia charge. (For an empty jelly jar?) He then proceeded to tell me that he was giving me a ticket for open container because the bottle was within arm's reach. (Absolutely impossible).

Officer Cox finally spoke to me and said "We have given you lots of information and I want for you to answer one for me" "If you are what you say you are why you do bare tattoos and what do they represent"

I said thank you officer I will respond the best way I know how.

I have eighteen large red ants that go from my ankle to my belly button and it's a joke to make people laugh and draw them to me. (It is a reminder that when it's all done I will be an ant bed). Next on my right forearm I bare an angiogram of the words Life and Death which represent that although I may appear as death I am really Light. I then told him that on my right shoulder I bore the banner of a US Army soldier over the unit crest of a 13 Foxtrot because I am a forward observer. (a fist with a lightning bolt representing God's judgment on the wicked after the ancient order of Saint Barbara). I then told him that below that was an image of seven different guitars representing the fact that I was a master guitar player and I used my talent to draw men to me. I then directed Officer Cox to my left forearm which bares a yellow warning sign with a curvy road on it to remind us that there would be dangerous roads ahead and that we should proceed with caution. On my left shoulder I bare the names of my children and another guitar. (Sorry no cool meaning this time) I asked them if they would like for me to remove my shirt and show them my last tattoo and they complied. I removed my shirt exposing another angiogram located between my shoulder blades and I said "I bare the mark of the illuminati diamond, it represents the four elements of science and it is my heritage because I am the son of a Mason that is the son of a Mason dating all the way back to the knights Templar and that I was a Master Mason.

Officer Lightfoot rudely told me to put my shirt back on. I was completely courteous and respectful and I did not understand why officer Lightfoot was angry with me or why he treated my office as a public servant with such disrespect. He must hate Pastors.

Officer Lightfoot then handed me quite possibly the most inaccurate ticket ever created and explained to me that he still didn't know what was really up but that he was going to let me off easy and not charge me with the pot (which was not mine and disappeared as quickly as it had magically appeared in the first place) but that I would receive a drug paraphernalia charge and an open container charge because my wine bottle (a pastors communion wine) was within arm's reach (aprox. six feet away). I thanked him for his time and asked him if the exemption of the drug paraphernalia law didn't state that if I manufactured smoking products I could have them with me during the course of my business and Officer Lightfoot told me " If seek any course of action against this ticket I will personally seek vengeance upon you and I will put you in jail at any time in the next two years and that every person that was ever caught with pot in his town would be immediately arrested (The Law) and that it would be my fault". I thanked him for squaring me away, took my ticket and got the heck out of there as soon as I could.

Both squad cars should have video and audio

(but you won't find lightfoot's)

Now my professional analysis of the officers as a Pastor, Teacher, counselor, and a Senior Drill instructor's personal assistant at the FATC at Fort Sill follows.

Officer Cox is squared away. The only deficiency in his dress and appearance was a cross proudly displayed on his uniform (violation of dress code). He was courteous, respectful and professional and respected the public office that I held.

Officer Lightfoot is what we soldiers call a dirt bag. His footwear was not spit shined, his uniform was not well kept, His candor was that of a bar room brawler, he was disrespectful to my public office, He called me a liar, If I did have pot I should have been arrested on the spot and if I did not have pot then how could an empty jelly jar be drug paraphernalia. By my observations he cannot write, he cannot spell, he does not know where he is at, he does not know the speed limit, he cannot tell time, he cannot tell the difference between solid black and grey in fact he cannot even spell grey (GRAY), he cannot dictate information properly (1796 Ford ?). He cannot judge height, he does not know direction. He does not know Texas law, and he does not know his job.

In Summery I feel that officer Lightfoot is a complete disgrace to his uniform and all of the fine men and women that serve as law enforcement officers. I feel that he should be suspended without pay until a complete internal investigation has occurred and after due process of law I hope that he is permanently disbarred from law enforcement forever.

With all due respect

Rev. Nathon Quinn Dees

CEO and Founder Three Dees Associates

The Next day Aaron and I went back to Investigate and the Sherriff in Franklin told us "You will not find the Truth that you seek here, You must look elsewhere" and I saw that he bore the Square and Compass and I said "Thank you Brother" and left as fast as my Old Ford Betsy could move and drove straight to the DPS Headquarters.

I had been asked to go pick up a motorcycle for a friend and I was driving across Texas to get it when I started having highway hypnoses in the middle of the day for no apparent reason. I was passing out while I was driving during the middle of the day for no apparent reason. I was drinking energy drinks to try and stay awake and slamming coffee. Nothing seemed to help. Finally I pulled over at a convenience store and I heard the words diabetic coma in my head so I went in and bought a gallon of distilled water and some jalapeño peppers to counter act the effects of what was happening to me. I went outside and walked to the back of the store where I forced myself to throw up. I regurgitated almost strait sugar from all of the energy drinks and my body was shutting down. I walked up and down the drive way for nearly an hour before I had stabilized my condition enough to drive again. I then proceeded to the grocery store where I went to the pharmacy and explained to the pharmacist that I was a former combat lifesaver medic from the Army and what conditions I was treating myself for and I bought enough over the counter medicine to save my own life. I called the paramedics and they arrived nearly forty five minutes later. They checked all of my vitals and explained to me that I basically knew more about what was happening to me that they did and that there was really nothing more that they could do for me so the y released me and I went on my way.

I made it to Austin where I got my friend Matt Cool to drive me back home to Bryan where I would seek help to find out what was really happening to me the next day. The following morning Aaron left for Austin to take Matt back home and I went to get some help for my condition.

I wanted a pet scan to check the levels of serotonin in my brain because I thought that I has Serotonin Toxicity Syndrome so I contacted the University first so that I could get a referral to the local MHMR where I could get sent to a hospital for the PET scan at no cost to me since there was no VA facility in Bryan.

Chapter Seven
Government Sanitarium from Hell

This was a big mistake. The girl at A&M that I talked to had been my councilor before and was another cookie cutter psychologist so when I described to her in great detail what had happened to me and why I was there she basically betrayed me and sold me out. She sent a letter to the MHMR that said I was confused and having troubling thoughts which was a complete and total lie so when I arrived for help I was met with a level of opposition that I would have never expected in a million years. Since I was a U.S. Army veteran and had mental illness they assessed that I was a danger to myself and to society. Since they did not know who I was they thought that I was delusional when I told them that I was a former pastor and that I owned a business. They did not believe anything that I said because I was a mental patient. I had been sent to school by the VA to receive training to become a peer support specialist for the mentally ill and I was actually a councilor at the VA working as a mediator between the doctors and patients. I had been in college studying psychology and had authored a book on mental illness and I was a thirteen foxtrot U.S. Army veteran that had received combat lifesaver training as a medic and I had completed water utility safety school at Texas A&M.

Everything that I told them was completely true and accurate but they did not care. They did not check out my story. They did not call my doctor. They arrested me against my will and sent me to a CIA maximum security psycho ward on the sixth floor of the Michael DeBakey VA Hospital in Houston and I was now a prisoner. Hell, I thought that I was going to the hospital for a pet scan I had no Idea that I was being arrested. I went in for help. I was articulate, calm, I knew exactly what I was talking about and I had proof of everything that I had said but no one wanted to hear what I had to say.

I was some U.S. Army violent psycho that needed to be incarcerated because I was dangerous. This was my reward for a life of service to my country and community. I had no arrest record, I had never been in a fight and I had spent my whole life in servitude to the church, my country, and my community and I was doing it again.

I was under contract to buy a church and start a school, not hurt other people or myself but that is not the way that they saw me. I was manic. I was dangerous. I was out of control. I was delusional. Well it turns out that I must have been completely delusional for ever asking anyone for help in the first place because the cause and effect of going to doctors for help completely destroyed my life and left me homeless and broke.

Chapter Eight
No Honor for Heroes

When I arrived at the hospital I was arrested, stripped of everything that I owned and confined to a cell. I didn't understand what was going on yet and I did not know why they just didn't give me an x ray and send me home. No one ever checked me or treated me for the condition that had nearly cost me my life and since it was on a Friday I would not even see a real doctor until the following Monday. It took until one AM before they finally in processed me and took me to my quarters. By this time I had realized what was going on and I had asked for a pen and paper to start taking notes so I could document what was being done to me.

So two days before I was free and I owned a business and I was an inventor and now I was a ward of the state under supervision for suicide and homicide and they were trying to force me to take meds against my will when I had been off of them for over a year under my doctors care. I was in complete recovery and I was a peer support technician that actually worked for the VA as a volunteer in Austin but here in Houston where they would not even call my doctor or check my records or anything.

They had miss diagnosed me and prescribed me meds after five minutes of interview. I told them that I was a holistic practitioner and that I used herbal medication and diet to control my condition and that in fact the two medicines that they had prescribed for me were not for the illness that I had and that they would counter act each other and endanger my life. It said it right on the drug information pamphlet that came with the medicine. The nurses said that if the prescriptions were wrong that you needed to tell the doctor, well I had not even seen a real doctor yet and they were trying to force me to take the wrong meds against my will. I felt as if this were some kind of weird conspiracy and that they were trying to kill me. I did what I was trained to do. I established my rank and position and set up a chain of command.

I found out who was the highest ranking soldier in the psycho ward and who was most capable of taking command of the situation. It was me once again. I was the only one that refused to take the crazy pills and I was the only one there that had not actually done anything wrong to myself or anyone else to get there. I was the only one that new the time and date and where I was and why I was there every one else was so drugged up that they did not know what was going on. Now that I was a pastor that basically gave me a commission and made me a chaplain so I posted my name, rank and position outside my door and I let them know that I was freemason. The next morning people had started writing their name and rank on my door so I could identify the people that were still sane and knew what was going on.

The next morning at chow I was directed to the officers table where I was briefed by a man named Kenny Roberts that said he was a three star general.

Hell, this was a psycho ward this guy could have been anyone but we had been stripped of all of our personal belongings and jewelry and shoes and everything when we were admitted and Kenny was wearing a two hundred fifty dollar Adidas jogging suit, Reeboks and a Rolex watch.

Kenny told me that everything was going to be alright and that I was not going to get out anytime soon or for at least seventy two hours and that I should just relax and make the best of it. So that Saturday morning I was seated at the officers table with a three star General on the sixth floor maximum security government controlled military psych ward because less than forty eight hours before I was dying on the side of the road, saved my own life and then went to a doctor to get an X-ray.

Chapter Nine
Hell on Earth

How could this possibly be happening to me? What did I do? Who did I piss off? Why was this happening to me?!

Ok so here is the score, It is Saturday morning, I am locked up in a maximum security military psycho ward, I can't see a doctor until Monday. They are trying to force me to take medication that I don't want and don't need. It's the week end so they cannot and will not call my real doctor Dr. Clayton. I haven't been in the military for over fourteen years and I'm in here with guys that just came off the front line in the Middle East with fucking bullet holes in their head that are completely whacked out. I am still very ill from whatever sickness that I had that got me here in the first place and no one will treat me for it. Alright Nathon, we have been in some fucked up situations before and I saw one flew over the koo koo's nest before so I know the game, let's play ball.

I asked for a felt tipped marker and some paper (You could not have a pen because you might kill someone with it) and I started taking notes and writing down everything that was happening to me and everyone else. Well that made me dangerous to them and pissed everyone off. So the fun began. I started interviewing everyone in there that I could actually hold a conversation with and helping out all the war heroes and combat veterans that were locked up for serving their country. Everyone knew who I was by noon chow and the lines were drawn. As always you either love Nathon or hate Nathon so I had basically divided the room into two camps. Those that were used to being railroaded by the system were telling me just to shut up and take the meds so that we could all get out and every one that understood what was happening were supporting me and telling me their own horror stories about this place.

I had a Navy seal that wanted to kill me, my roommate of course. There were Delta force Marines, Army Rangers, Navy Seals and elite Navy rescue guys. These people were hard core they had PTSD, Bi Polar disorder, Schizophrenia, drug and alcohol problems, suicidal tendencies, and not to mention homicidal tendencies. Hell, some of them were just getting a break from killing people on the front line in the Middle East. This was definitely not the local MHMR.

The place looked clean at first glance but by the time that you took a good look you could tell that things were unkept and unsanitary. They only cleaned the day room every couple of days and there was food all stuck to the tables and floors, the sinks didn't work in half of the rooms, and they were rewashing and reusing disposable plastic silverware. All of the linins smelt like septic like they were washed in waste water or something but they were definitely not clean. Most of all the war heroes and men and women that had lost their sanity serving their country and were scarred for life had fewer rights than a TDC prison inmate. You could not go outside, you could not take a walk, you could not do exercise or PT, there was no smoking, no newspapers, no decent reading material and if you so much as looked at a staff member wrong they would medicate you against your will and put you in a holding cell. There were E8 US Navy master chiefs scrubbing the floors and cleaning windows. This place was a disgrace and a dishonor to the fine men and women that had served our country. I have actually been in jails in third world countries that were better that the sixth floor of the Houston VA sixth floor maximum security psycho ward. Most of all we were being held prisoner for crimes that we did not commit.

When it came time to shave you stood in a line with the people that were allowed to shave and one at a time under supervision you were given one of those blue disposable open faced body razors that they use for surgery. Not even a safety razor. They were so bad that we had contest to see who could actually shave without cutting your face. Some of the guys looked like hamburger meat when they got through. I almost won the shaving contest once but a female sergeant found one speck of blood on my face and I got beat by a marine. We were the only ones that were not bleeding profusely. One of the saddest moments for me was watching the red blood of a U.S. Marine pour down his face into the sink while he tried to shave with this surgical ball razor. What a fucking dishonor, what a fucking disgrace. Some of the men were completely incoherent and just shuffled up and down the hall completely whacked out of their minds on psych drugs others were under guard and not allowed to leave their rooms. They were more or less there permanently and that was their goal for me. To fuck me up on meds bad enough so that I would become incoherent and they could keep me there forever. It was not going to happen to me. Fuck them. I refused to take the meds and I refused to even where my ID or arm band. The first thing that I noticed when they put the arm band on me was that it had my whole social security number printed on it in large bold print. I ripped it off and told them that they were fucking crazy if they thought that they could publicly display my social security number on my arm and that it was a violation of HIPA, the freedom of information act and it violated my civil rights as an American. They said well you can't have your meds unless you have an arm band and I told them they could stick them up their ass with their fucking arm band because I was not going to take their poison and I was not going to wear the arm band when my social security number was on it. Everyone saw my defiance and realized that they had a choice too and started refusing the wrong medications and asking for a doctor to review their cases. I was causing them way more trouble than I was worth. By shift change and evening chow I had already turned the place upside down and everyone there knew who I was. I was still seated at the officers table with Crazy Kenny the three star general and I had started giving away all of my food. I don't drink milk so I gave it away, I don't eat deserts so I gave it away, I don't eat white bread so I gave it away and I don't eat sugar so I gave it away. In fact there was very little nutritional value in any of the meals they were serving and the food sucked so I started giving mine away to everyone else. It was like an auction. "Hey Dees what do you want to get rid of" well I don't eat this and I don't like that and this has no nutritional value hell take it all I could use a fast for a couple of days. By the time I left I had everyone in the day room sharing their food and giving up what they did not need.

It was almost as if I reminded them that we were all soldiers and that we were all in this together and that we had to stick together and pull our resources in order to survive.

That day after chow it happened. We were sitting at the table when Crazy Kenny who was at least six foot four and had curly flaming red hair with blue eyes started singing Beatles songs at random. Well it was on. He started drumming on the table and we started singing every classic rock song that we knew for hours but Kenny loved the Beatles and we sang them nearly every time we got together after that. One day we busted out a Beatles song in the middle of the hall way right in front of the nurses' station and did it so bad ass that when we finished the guards stopped what they were doing and came and listened. One of them even shook my hand afterward and told that I was great. Kenny would do the Paul McCartney parts and I would be John Lennon and our harmonies were pretty good. We were both singers and professional musicians that had played in bands and sang for years so we really enjoyed singing in the nut house.

Chapter Ten
Meeting Dr. Do Little

Finally I get assigned to the head psychiatrist Dr. Hartly Little. When he interviewed me he asked what my trade was. I told him that I was a Master Mason, Master Craftsman and that I knew all commercial and residential trades. He wrote " Mr. Dees is obviously delusional and thinks that he can do anything" I told him that I had the license to prove everything that I said and that in fact I had more license than his whole staff. Here is the problem Dr. Little. You spent your whole life and all of your daddy's money to learn one trade and you have about a 120 IQ and can only do one thing. I have a GED and I can do anything and I have around 160 IQ and it pisses you off. "Mr. Dees has severe Axis two Narcissistic Personality Disorder and I recommend that he be permanently institutionalized by the State of Texas". I said you want to put me in the state home!
That is very Funny Dr. Do Little because Ron Pfiser the head of the Peer Support program tried to hire me to work there at the recommendation of Dr Clayton at the Austin VA and I am a licensed Peer Support Specialist dumbass!

Well after that he made some calls and actually talked to Dr. Clayton that confirmed to him that everything that I had told him was the truth and that I had been under her care and worked at the VA for NAMI and that I was a genius and perfectly fine and that she had me off of the meds. Realizing that he was in a completely fucked up situation he found a loop hole. Since he did not know the special circumstances that the Army gave me for discharge, when he saw that I only had 18 months of active duty service he yanked all of my VA benefits and billed me $ 15,000.00 for a six day stay against my will. Then he filled on social security to garnish my Government check to pay the VA back for six days of hell under involuntary incarceration and threw me out in the street to be homeless and broke and destroy my life.

Chapter Eleven
WTF Could Possibly Happen Next?

Aaron had taken all of our most valuable possessions, like my 74 Stratocaster, My father's 1914 Silver Anniversary H.N. White trumpet, my Marshall amps and my George Snydo Original Print and put them in the Pawn shop for safe keeping and get some gas money to come get me from Houston where Dr. Little had just thrown me out onto the street. This turned out to be very wise because by the time that we got back to College Station our house had been broke into three times, Guy had moved out and took all of his shit and moved into a FEMA trailer, Chris had stole my electronic Drum Set and filled false charges on me and Aaron claiming the equipment was his and their friend the Land Lord had given me a fake city eviction order and filled false charges on me. Guy's friend Nathan Winchester who was my old land Lord that I had done some work for filled false breaking and entering charges against me and Guy's friend Justin Murphy filled false Kidnapping charges on me because his daughter ran away and was hiding in the woods and I had absolutely nothing to do with any of this. Some other College Kids from A&M had stole my CNC machine prototype and all of Aaron's video games, filled false charges claiming the stuff was his and my ex wife Athea had filed restraining orders against me and it had been a Year since I even saw her and she lived 150 miles away and my two step sons never spoke to me again. Nearly every family member had blocked me and unfriended me and changed their e mails and phone numbers and my best friends rejected me and shut Aaron and I out.

The only person in College Station that would even talk to me or shake my hand was Bill Allen from the Harry Bikers TV show, on the History Channel, who was a friend of mine.

 Bill looked me strait in the eye and told me that the only thing that I had done wrong was be different and that I needed to get out of town immediately. We said a short prayer and I left. Chris Text Aaron and told us that there was an APB to arrest both of us on site if we came anywhere near Texas A&M. I was brought in for questioning three times of the next few days and by the time that I finally had a detective look at everything he was absolutely amazed to learn that there was absolutely no evidence to any of the charges and that I had been the victim of a highly elaborate plot by my friends and suggested that I leave College Station ASAP so I did.
Who would have thought that Texas A&M and College Station were the CIA New World Order Headquarters for Monsetto and Homeland security Marshall law Civil Terrorism training.

 We ended up living in a gutted abandoned trailer house at my friends Tim Butler's house in Houston. Before we could get settled or regroup there the trailer was broken into and my Marshall amps and the rest of my tools were stolen so we packed up the few things that we had left and headed for Austin. When we got to Austin my friend Sean Pollard let us move in the Barn in his back yard in exchange for working on it and Aaron and I started to rebuild once more with absolutely nothing.

Chapter Twelve
Then Things got even Weirder
As if that was even possible

I had done some jobs for Sean and made some money, my Buddy Jimmy down the street let me rent his house with no money down if I remodeled it for him so Aaron and I got our own place and he got a job and we started over again. Something was happening to me and my perceptions and understanding of this great conspiracy were all coming to light. I was doing much research about ten hours a day reading about ascension and the pineal gland and crystals and holistic healing. I learned about Chakras and meditation from my friend Summer Walters. I learned about the Book of Enki and the writings of Zecheria Sitchen. I read the Emerald Tables of Thoth and Hermes Thrise Greate, I learned the virtues of Pathogarus, The Gnostic Gospels from the Nag Hammad library. I learned about Nassim Harameim and sacred geometry. I built a pyramid in my back yard out of tube steel and started harnessing zero point energy. I was on fire again.

I was meditating at my desk and the voice spoke to me and told me to go treasure hunting so I went out prospecting in the creek. While down in the creek bed looking for signs of place gold I heard " Find the Ore Find the gold" and as soon as I heard that is looked down and picked up a strange piece of brown ore and took it home to research it. Well, It turns out that I had moved into the Strewn field of the Comet that hit the Gulf Coast sixty million years before and killed the dinosaurs. I found 120 lbs of the rarest Stony Iron Achondrite meteorite. They passed every test and they were radioactive, non magnetic, non conductive, and were 94% pure iron crystal carbonate black diamond inside with fusion crust and Regmaglyphs outside. Regular stony Iron sold for $50 a gram on the internet and some HED Achondrites were up to $500 a gram meaning that I had just found around Two and a half million dollars worth of meteorites.

Chapter Thirteen
Cock blocked Again

My friend had Just Got his P.E. degree from the University of Texas and worked for the State Department of Transportation as an engineer. He and his colleagues from work proved my theory and verified that they were meteorites for me but could not offer me the proper validation that I needed to make a sell. Another is a machinist and welder and his father is a Professor of metallurgy and we all knew that they were meteorites but not a single University or museum would validate my find even though they could not prove that I was not right. This one asshole at the North Texas State observatory could not debunk me and when he exposed it to the Geiger counter to prove that it was not radioactive and the Geiger counter went off he said "Well this is an old Geiger counter and it is probably malfunctioning". I told him that he was full of shit and explained to him how that a Geiger counter was nothing more than an anode with a speaker and an analog current transformer and that he was a fucking idiot. Then he tried to tell me that it was hematite and I told him that hematite had a melting point of 1500 Degrees Fahrenheit and I whipped out my mini torch and showed them that it just started getting red at 2000 degrees F. Three Museums and three Universities and everyone that I talked to knew less about meteorites than I did. I was so pissed off over this. My P.E. friend took his information and samples and went to the McDonald observatory in West Texas as an academic and asked them point blank if this whole meteorite thing was a scam to control the market. The man looked at my friends hand and saw the square and Compass. The answer was Yes. They told him that since no one can actually swear that something is a meteorite unless it is a documented fall of a typical known type and that the Scammers like the Meteorite Men Show were there to create a false market for the commodities and only validate the ones that they or their colleagues found.

Chapter Fourteen
Enough is Enough

In addition to the Stony Irons I had identified at least six different other meteorites in the creek and collected them as well as Crystallized Calcite Alomasaurus teeth, Megalodon teeth. I also found Precifincterus fossils in the same creek proving that my theory about the source of the meteors was correct. All of the normal people were getting angry with me and were mad because I had discovered these things and no one but the few smart people that I knew understood that I was right and I lost several good friends over this. They would actually say that I was too smart to believe this and that it was embarrassing them to see me this way so I told them to get the Fuck out of my house.
 Nearly every single person that I knew in Austin was hooked on Smoking Methamphetamines, Shooting Meth, or taking Adoral.

 They all were suffering from Meth induced Schizophrenia and their ego identities would attack me at random and I was understanding the great negative forces that had been set against me here because I was in Fact a chosen one and an RH negative hybrid from a royal knights Templar blood line. It all started making since to me.

 I was the reincarnation of an Ascended Master. My First name is from AkhenNaton "The son of Aton" and In Ancient Hebrew Nathon means a continual giving gift of God. My middle name id Quinn which is Gaelic for intelligence and Royalty under refuge and Dees is Scottish and means Descendants of King David from the Davidson clan. I am from the CulDees of Iona Scotland and I had no idea about any of this before. When I studied the CulDees I found that they taught and believed the same exact principals and theory that I had developed on my own called the "Quaternary". In fact the Tattoo of the Illuminate diamond on my back was an ancient symbol of my clan representing the four elements of science. CulDees is from Chaldeans and means Worshipers of God. I was the incarnation of an ancient astronomer priest from a clan of Masonic Warrior monks.

Chapter Fifteen
Good by New World Order
Hola Costa Rica
Tuanis Pura Vida

As soon as my lease was up I gave away all of my equipment. I Left some stuff with my sister, Packed up every single rock, stone, meteorite and fossil then drove to Florida to find my brother Damon who had been clean and sober and on his own now for seven years since he was deported from Costa Rica. I put all of my treasures in a secret location in Miami and I flew back to Jaco, Costa Rica to live with and care for my father who was now blind.
I gave Damon my Ford truck and my tools so that he could provide for himself and Pop and I flew home back to where I felt safe and Aaron would follow us shortly. When I got to Jaco my friend Mr. Woods that owned my Hostel building had a house that had been damaged by thieves and left vacant so I remodeled it completely In two weeks and did such a good job that Floyd told me that he intended to hold the real estate for ten more years and that I could have the house to live in for free until we decided to sell the property.

All I know is that I was home and that I had no intentions what so ever of ever returning to the Unites States of Confusion. I was Home and Byron and I were so happy to have escaped from the American New World Order Death machine. There were many more adventures ahead for me in Costa Rica and I was ready to finish my ascension and enter into my Shamnistic role as an El Elehido "Chosen one" and a Reike healer.

By this time I was so in tune with my inner dialog that I was discovering new things almost daily.

The first thing that I did was discover over a thousand fossils of Triangular conical teeth from a 200 million year old Archosaurus Crocomorph that I named the Jacosoraus Costaricus, after my town.

Next, I found ten different types of semi precious minerals that wash up on the beach at random on certain days.

I collect hundreds of pounds of Chalcedony Crystal quartz, celestial quartz, Agate, Smokey Quartz, Rose Quartz, Amber Quartz, Heliotrope Bloodstone and fossilized Dinosaur poop.

It's like, I'm the only person that ever even noticed them all over the beach. It's like treasure hunting every day. I had discovered ley lines with my dowsing rods and the energies here were off the scale so I built a new pyramid and set 120 lbs of Quartz in it in the shape of a pyramid and then put meteorites on the top and it started creating so much power that my body literally jolts when I touch it and It ignites my Chakras and my appendages all start vibrating as my crown and Third eye Chakras open up and my Pineal gland starts producing DMT.

I had started my next incarnated manifestation as

"The Guru AkhNathon "An Ascended Master and teacher of higher consciousness.